REVEALING
SECRETS
TO BREAKING
BAD HABITS

REVEALING SECRETS TO BREAKING BAD HABITS

David Sangster

To order additional copies of this book, contact:
Xlibris Corporation
1-888-795-4274
www.Xlibris.com
Orders@Xlibris.com
52475

CONTENTS

PART ONE: Character Building Principles............ 11

What You Commit To Become You 12
The Danger Of Idolatry 15
Becoming God-Like 16
Created To Be God-like 19
You Are Work-in-Progress 20
It's Evolution..21
Be Humble..23
Practice Self-Discipline 24
Be Willing to Surrender....................................26
The Transforming Power of Forgiveness 28
Move Beyond Your Past 30

PART TWO: Renewing Your Mind........................ 33

Renewing Your Mind 33
It's All in Your Mind 34
Have You Lost Your Mind? 37
Every Thought Yields Something of Its Kind.............38
What You Say..39
Trouble in My Mind 41

PART THREE: Defeating Temptation 43

How Temptation Works 44
Divert Your Attention......................................46
Recognize Your Pattern....................................47
Grab A Friend 49
Pray For Help...51
Run For It! 53

PART FOUR: You Are What You Eat 55

What's Eating You? 56
Don't Eat That 58
What's For Supper? 60
What Goes In Must Come Out 63
Benefit of Exercise 64

Introduction

This book presents revealing secrets to breaking bad habits as a truth to be accepted and a fact to be understood rather than an opinion to be debated or an option to be considered.

> You shall know the truth and the truth shall make you free.
> (John 8:32)

To make free is a process of producing and transforming. The truth will transform you. Some say the truth will set you free. But to set free and to make free are two different kinds of freedom. To be set free does not involve a transformation. Only the truth has the power to transform. Spiritual growth is the process of replacing lies with truth. *To make free* is the process of transforming a person's mental makeup.

> People need more than bread for their life, they must feed on
> the "principle" of truth. (Matthew 4:4 NLT)

God is the truth that makes us free. He is the source of truth, the perfect standard of what is right. He frees us from the consequences of bad habits and other forms of bondage.

When we, as believers, make a commitment to entrust our lives on the promises, power, and principles of God, we are still living in hostile territory that is under the influence and power of Satan and our flesh.

I have discovered that every bad habit starts with you and to end a bad habit starts with you. You are the catalyst. You must first conceive in consciousness what you desire because everything begins with a thought. Not all habits are bad. I want to focus on the bad ones because they are the most detrimental. Anything that's detrimental shouldn't be viewed as sentimental—that which is governed by feelings or emotions rather than thought or reason. If you have a bad habit, you are the reason why it still exists. It still exists because you have been sentimental with it. The longer you are sentimental with it, the longer you will be castigated by it.

Unfortunately, some people will tolerate a bad habit simply because they feel powerless and choose to be defeated instead of getting treated. You don't have to be castigated as long as you are motivated. As long as you believe it, you can achieve it. As a man thinks in his heart, so is he. As long as you believe you can be free and move in the direction of freedom, you will be free. But freedom has a price. As long as you pamper and cater to a bad habit, the longer it will dominate you. Here are some news you can use:

> The weapons of our warfare are not carnal, but mighty through God to the pulling down of strongholds, casting down vain imagination and every high thing that exalt itself against the principles of God and every thought to the obedience of Christ. (2 Corinthians 10:4-5)

You must understand that we are in the midst of a war of the mind. And victory cannot be obtained without the proper principles, methods, and strategies. The apostle Paul teaches us to put on the whole armor of God because, like it or not, we are engaged in a battle that starts from birth to the time of departure from earth: there is no quarter given, no cease-fire, no holds barred, no temporary truce, no cessation of hostilities. From this time forward, there is all-out war. The apostle Paul said the true nature of this war is against the world, your flesh, and the devil. Your life is constantly being driven by something, whether it's fear, doubt, confusion, forgiveness, hate, guilt, envy, jealously, lying, etc.

The devil is very cunning and tries to oppress and depress you through your thought pattern, other people, and difficult circumstances in which the unaware are led into chains of bondage and other forms of captivity. However, God has not left us defenseless. He has provided principles and a greater power to overcome. If you rely on your own strength or your own personal opinions, you will fall into an endless pattern of defeat—oftentimes, unpleasant defeat. The real battle starts in the mind.

Perhaps you are one of those who grew up in a dysfunctional home devoid of divine principles, and as a result, you lack self-esteem, self-confidence, self-control, and certain people skills that are essential for strong character. Don't shortchange yourself and become complacent. We can do nothing of lasting significance apart from God. A weak, undeveloped character is a character that is in a crisis. To transform your character out of a crisis, you must take on the character of Christ. To be like Christ requires a mental and spiritual transformation of character. The only thing God gives us outside of salvation is opportunity. When opportunity knocks, don't make excuses. To make excuses is to speak the language of losers. What language will you speak, victory or defeat?

To you. If you're searching for change in your behavior and your life, this book is for you. I hope and pray that this book benefit you in more ways than one and will meet all your expectations by faith and actions. Faith without actions is fruitless faith.

Here's what the scripture says about faith:

- We walk by it.
- We live by it.
- We overcome the world by it.
- We are declared righteous by it.
- We are healed by it.
- We are forgiven by it.
- We are empowered by it.

Faith is God's work in you that changes you and gives new birth. It changes our hearts and attitudes. It is a living, creative, active substance that brings about change.

I am grateful to God and all my close-knit mentors for helping to shape and transform my life. You know who you are. Today, I take privilege in sharing this fruitful, life-changing wisdom with you. I share it with you as it was revealed to me by the Holy Spirit and my very own personal experience.

Part One

Character-Building Principles

Principles are comprehensive fundamental laws, doctrines, rules, or codes of conduct. Like the perfect ingredients, they exhibit or impart a characteristic quality for living.

Principles are essential for life. According to biblical scriptures, we are born without them. However, they are used to build or reconstruct our character, to enhance our way of life, and to improve our behavior. We all come here with jagged edges and cracks in our character. However, these divine principles are used to smooth out the jagged edges and seal up the cracks in our character. Your character is made up of the attributes that make up and distinguish an individual from others.

We are transformed by truth. These divine principles have the power to break bad habits, generate life, heal hurts, create faith, clean our mind, build character, and enhance our way of life. This is what truth will do for you.

Some people say, "The truth will set you free." But to be set free is not real freedom. To be set free is like a setback because there's no true transformation. There's a difference between *set free* and *made free*. To be *made free* means there's a process of shaping and growing and improving. What have you been improving on lately? Have you been set free or made free?

Whatever you don't want in your life can be eliminated from your life. Using the right principles, strategies, and methods is the key. Some habits we are born with while others are developed by repetition. Repetition is the mother of character and skill. To become great at something means you must rehearse it over and over again. Building character and improving skills is no exception. You must acquire what you desire.

Michael Jordan did not become one of NBA's best basketball players by sitting underneath a coconut tree ravenously eating coconuts. He did not become one of the league's best by lounging in his living room, munching on Orville Redenbacher's while watching *Days of Our Lives* all day, every day. Moreover, the William sisters did not become the world's best female tennis players by basking in the sun on Miami's sandy white beaches every day. They literally lived and breathed tennis. In fact, they spent six hours a day, six days a week at a very young age, practicing on the tennis court. How's that for commitment? There's more to come on that subject. However, we should place a higher premium on building our character instead of fame or wealth. Otherwise, our character will suffer from malnutrition because whatever you fail to feed will die. Moreover, whatever you commit to becomes you. If you commit to bad habits, unfruitfulness will be your reward. The reason why you're hooked on what you are hooked on is because you made a commitment, whether you realize it or not. God's ultimate goal for your life is not comfort, but character development (Ephesians 4:24 MSG).

What You Commit to Becomes You

Commitment is a faithful vow to a particular course of action. It is the state or instance of being obligated or emotionally impelled to a course.

I can't think of anything more powerful and more impacting that will form and shape your life more than the principle of commitment. What you commit to becomes you. What you commit to will either enhance your life or destroy your life. Tell me what you are committed to and I'll tell you what you are becoming. What are you committed to? Wait a minute! Hold that thought! You may say, "I'm not committed to anything." Then that's what you will become—nothing. Oops! There it is. If you never commit to anything in life, then your life will be like a ship at high seas without a rudder, drifting through life with no direction or sense of purpose. Everyone was created for a specific purpose. Knowing your purpose gives meaning to your life. Without God, life has no purpose; and without purposes, life has no meaning. Without meaning, life has no hope. Poor, pitiful you—what are you going to do?

The time and attention that you give to something or someone will form and shape your life unlike anything else. In fact, commitment plays a huge part in our lives. Wherever there's commitment, there's development.

Here are some examples: If you commit to booze, you will become a boozer, staggering your way through life. Not good!

1. If you commit to gossip, you will become a gossiper on the go.
2. If you commit to taking things that are not yours, you will become a kleptomaniac.
3. If you commit to gambling, you will become a gambler and will risk losing everything you have, including the shirt off your back, your dog, and your cat.
4. If you commit to prostitution, you will become a prostitute on the prowl.
5. If you commit to pornography, you will become a perverted pornographer.
6. If you commit to drugs, you will become a drug addict, and your life will become a drag.
7. If you commit to strip clubs, you will eventually be clubbed with a club at the club.
8. If you commit to unhealthy eating, you will be unhealthy. Disease will befall you.
9. If you commit your life and time to Christ, you will become Christlike. Whatever you commit to becomes a part of you. Consider this your forewarning.
10. If you commit to bad company, bad company is what you will become. That's why if you are trying to overcome something, you should always be aware of your surroundings. You shouldn't flow with bad company. Bad company corrupts good manners. Here are some more facts: Every day we encounter and interact with countless numbers of people—coworkers, neighbors, preying predators, stalkers, and wolves in sheep's clothing. Perhaps the most dangerous ones are the ones dressed like the chameleon who are hard to spot. They camouflage themselves in the presence of others just to protect their identity. I'm talking about those night-stalking, cunning, manipulative predators whose agenda is to rob you of your control. They are the sweet talkers. They appear to be kind and loving and speak flattering words and make promises that never come true. They take advantage

of your need to be loved and understood and manipulate you into doing what they want you to do. They are the false friends who lead you to believe that they are acting in your best interest when in fact they are not. They will actually school you.

Perhaps you are thinking about getting married. Marriage is a commitment. The person you marry will either enhance you or embarrass you. When it comes to marriage, you should seek for true love and for someone who will enhance and advance your life. Even if they are gifts from God, it does not mean every day is going to be a holiday. You may have to ask yourself, "What is this relationship doing to me and for me?" You can dream as big as you want and fly as high as the eagle, but if you marry a hell mate instead of your soul mate, you and all your hopes and dreams could end up in a hellhole, wondering, "How did I get here?" Find out if that person is a gift from God or a gift from the devil before you say, "I do." There comes a time in a person's life when he or she should say, "Enough is enough. I will not stay on this merry-go-round way of life.

I have discovered many people move from one bad relationship to another. This is because of a lack of commitment. You have to go on the inside of yourself and change something, including your people skills. You have to get rooted and grounded in love. If not, your character will never be developed. In fact, you cannot make progress without oppositions. Oppositions are simply competition for your transition. Just because there's a bump in the road does not mean you should bail out. Bumps serve as tests. If you are never tested, how will you know what level you are on? Stop bailing out! Bailing out is nothing more than copping out.

One reason why most people don't stay married is because they just cannot stand to be pressured. You have to understand that if you're always running from trouble when trouble arises, you will never become developed. Oppositions come to make you stronger. To get to the diamonds, you have to dig deep down, and that requires work and effort on your part. Even diamonds are developed under heat and periods of pressure. If you cannot stand heat and pressure, you will jump from one relationship to another, leaving you undeveloped. I realize there are some conditions: If you marry a psycho who beats you and never shows you respect, it's time to pack your bags. However, people today are getting a divorce because a rat is in the house. That's ridiculous! If they see a rat, they literally leave the house. If you are going to leave the house, go down to Walmart or Walgreens and purchase a rattrap. Oftentimes, when a rat sees you, he will turn and run. It doesn't make sense for you and the rat to run. These kinds of people lack commitment. And in retrospect, you will see that they have a *frog* mentality. What do I mean by that? They spend most of their time and life jumping. I'm not talking about jumping jacks. I'm talking about jumping from oppositions every time they are confronted with a problem. The longer you keep jumping from oppositions, the longer it will take you to make your transition.

You have to be considerate of other people's needs and desires. Not everything has to always go your way. It's not all about you. If you continue to do the same thing over and over and expect a different result, you are wasting your time. Where there's no reformation, there's no transformation. Life is about holding on and letting go. What are you holding on to? What are you willing to let go to make yourself a better man or woman? Stop being duped! Where there's no commitment, there's no development.

In today's world, many people don't want to commit to anything worthwhile. In today's world, I've seen more people who are committed to their cell phones more than any lifelong commitment. Some people will fight you about their cell phones. Hold up! Wait a minute! Anything you treasure or cherish more than God is idolatry. I didn't say, "Dollar tree." There are some things that you will not find at the dollar tree. Beware! There are many things that can become your idol.

The Danger of Idolatry

When you reject God from your life and affairs, he calmly backs down and excuses himself from your life, and the results can be devastating. The United States and many other nations are slowly being duped into idolatry. Harry Potter is a cult. That's right. And many are injecting this poison into the minds of our children, and we think it is OK. It's not OK! What you commit to becomes a part of you. Humanism is idolatry. Humanism is a rejection of God and focuses only on an individual's dignity, worth, and capacity. Humanism says, "I'm the captain of my own life!" Baby, you cannot take your next breath unless God gives it to you. Socialism is idolatry. Socialism is your dependence upon the state to take care of you. It is a system or condition of society in which the means of the distribution of goods are owned and controlled by the state. There may come a time when you may have to lean on the state. But don't lean too long. God is your unlimited source. But we have placed the state in the place where God should be. Many have made the state their god. You shouldn't want to be controlled by man. This is leading to the mark of the beast (666). The mark of the beast is a satanic mark that man must take on or accept in order to buy or sell anything in the very near future. In fact, that system is already in progress. The number of the beast is the number of man (Revelation 13:17-18). What you commit to controls you. Don't sell your soul for a piece of gold.

Money can be an idol. Some people don't just make money; they make money their god. Money makes the world go round, but a lack of money will shut it down. Think about it. Our currency reads, "In God We Trust." Many people don't see it that way. Instead of trusting God, they trust in their currency. They literally destroy their health trying to obtain wealth and end up spending all their wealth trying to maintain their health. How dumb is that? The cure is not in your currency. Worshipping or idolizing anything other than God could be a sign that you don't believe you are valuable. God wants to be the center of your attention. If you have been redeemed, you are now the recipient of God the Father's unmerited favor through Christ. God wants to be the center of your attention. His desire is that you become more like him and not more like money.

Becoming Godlike

This does not pertain to the physical aspect or nature but to his spiritual and moral nature. You may ask, "How are we like God?" Here's how:

1. We have a moral consciousness.
2. We can discern right and wrong.
3. We can think and reason.
4. We can create.
5. We experience emotions.

Like God, we are spiritual beings wrapped in the physical. However, our spirits are immortal. It's very important to develop a daily habit of spending devotional time with him because he wants to be involved in every area of your life, including conversations, problems, activities, and even your thoughts. In fact, this is one of our greatest privileges, and we should take advantage of it. Spending time with God is the best way to move into his presence. The Bible says, "In His presence is the fullness of joy" (Psalms 16:11). *Fullness* implies the inclusion of everything that is wanted or required by something that can be held, contained, or attained by it. These steps require commitment. If there's no time spent, there's no development. Commitment leads to fulfillment.

When you commit to God, you become more like God. Some people want to be like Mike. Who do you want to be like? Beware! Inside Mike you will find Ike. You, me, Ike, and Mike were created to be like Christ. Who's showing up in you? Hold that thought! Are you having an identity crisis? If so, let me help you out: divinity should be your identity.

The only reason why so many people have an identity crisis is because their character is in a crisis: they don't really know who they are. That's a sad state of affairs because someone can come along and declare that you are a nut, and you will believe it. There may be days when you may truly feel like a nut or a loser. But you're not a nut or a loser. God's ultimate goal for your life is to develop your current character into a Christlike character. This is your greatest privilege and ultimate destiny. Divine principles will reveal who you are and who you are supposed to be. When you don't know who you are, you will jump your way through life like a greasy grasshopper, with no sense of purpose or direction. Wait a minute! Where do you think you're going? If you don't know where you're going, you could end up in a hellhole. Open your eyes! Life is not a game of hide-and-seek. Take off that veil so you can keep your tail out of jail. Because when you don't know where you're going, you will always be guessing on your journey. And as a result, you will find yourself in the wrong jurisdiction.

When you do what you want to do, there are consequences. Bad choices and bad attitudes will lead you straight into retribution and prosecution.

I have discovered that there are two kinds of people: the self-centered and the God centered. Self-centered people always focus on themselves and want to be in control of their own lives and destinies, while God-centered people focus on the things of God. Which one are you?

God's ultimate goal for everyone is to take on his characteristics and become more and more like himself (Ephesians 4:24).

I've heard some people say, "I'm just trying to find myself." My question is, how do you know when you have found yourself? As long as you're looking for yourself, you will be looking for a mighty long time. The best thing you can do is to stop looking for yourself. As long as you are looking for yourself, you will always have an identity crisis. You will always be looking for somebody you cannot and will not find because only divinity is your identity. You were created in the image and likeness of Christ (God). However, you will lose that image when you choose to live life outside that image by living like how you want to live. If you could unzip yourself and step out to be someone else, who would you choose to be? If you are looking for yourself, look at Christ. Only when you find Christ is when you find yourself because you were created to be like Christ. Divinity is your identity. Divinity has been your identity since day one. Since that's the case, why do we choose to be someone else other than divinity? That's when you lose your identity. You lose your identity even when you don't know who you are. Who are you? Divinity is your identity.

We have the privilege to be equal with God. It's not blasphemy for us to consider ourselves equal with God. When God decided to reproduce himself, he created man. However, that likeness or image has nothing to do with this physical body. We are spiritual beings. Understanding the Godhead results as man develops an awareness of who he is. God is creating himself within us. His ultimate manifestation on earth is found in man. You and the Father are one. Think about that.

The real fall of man occurred when Adam and Eve fell short of their Godhead. They missed the mark. And whenever you miss the mark, you miss your chance to be equal with God. Jesus came, demonstrating what the first Adam was supposed to have been like and, at the same time, revealing what we are supposed to be like. Sin is failure to operate in oneness with God. Sin is missing the mark to be like God.

As believers, we are one with the Father. Even pharaoh saw himself as a god. He operated in otherness instead of oneness with the true God. Lucifer wanted to be like God. However, he made a big mistake when he wanted to be God. There can only be one God. To be equal with God does not mean to be perfect. Equality with God does not always mean sameness because we have the experience of sin.

The Bible says, "But he who unites himself with the Lord is one with Him" (1 Corinthians 6:17).

You were created in the image and likeness of God. You were not created in the likeness and image of your parents. They were only the vessels that God used to get you here. You may have some similar physical traits and characteristics, but that is not the ultimate image in which you were created. God's ultimate goal for your life is to be like himself.

Created to Be Godlike

Everything was created for a purpose—including the shoes on your feet, the clothes on your back, the car you drive, the chair you sit on, the phone you use to tell people off, the bed you sleep in, the house you live in, and the pen I'm using to write this book; all started out as a dream but is now manifested into reality and serves purpose. You were created to be like Christ; therefore, you have greatness within you.

Each person in the world carries a seed of greatness within them to deliver to the world. Many people have died, and many more will die without manifesting their seed of greatness because they have allowed other things to interfere with their purpose for being here. It's not good to go down with untapped treasures. Regardless of age, color, creed, or origin, you are here to live out a divine assignment. What's your assignment?

Your assignment is to do the things or work of God. Your purpose is to become godlike or like Christ. So please don't let any person or power stop you from becoming what you were destined to be. There is a power you were born to express in the earth. To become godlike, there are some things you must let go (Matthew 6:24). Remember, life is about holding on and letting go.

If you choose to hold on to human qualities perhaps it will be hard for divinity to show up in you. You have a power within your earthen vessel that is all-powerful and all-revealing. It will take shape when you learn to shift shape from your physical identity to your spiritual identity. Be transformed by God's truth and stop trying to carbon copy yourself after another. There may be individuals in your circle that have demonstrations of God, but abide in your gift and your calling, and as a result, you will be able to rise to the greatest height without becoming intimidated by someone else's ideology of God. It is not comparative when it comes to God. As long as God can find the light of truth in you, then you will emanate the luminance of truth that's required.

God's ultimate goal is to reconstruct your character into a Christlike character. Becoming Christlike is a continuous process. You have to make up your mind who's it going to be, you or God. One must choose to decrease in order for the other to increase. John said, "I must decrease that God may increase" (John 3:30). What will you do? God doesn't make robots.

If you cannot decrease in your sinful human nature, divinity cannot increase within you. When you take up your cross, that's when the human side dies. When you take up your cross, the old you gets lost. Divinity becomes your identity. God will only feed you what you hunger for. You must desire him to be the leader in your life to receive life and godliness, in order for you not to be controlled by the evil desires of your flesh. You must die to self to live unto God. You don't have to live a defeated life. However, falling does not make you a failure. Here's what you should know.

You Are a Work in Progress

Our lives are like an assembly line. The farther you get down the line, the more you are developed into the finished product. You are an unfinished product in progress. This process is a gradual process.

There's an old song that goes "please be patient with me / God is not through with me yet." That's because you are on life's assembly line, and your development takes time. In fact, God can do it instantly, but he has chosen to do it gradually.

Paul wrote, "We are sojourners and pilgrims traveling through life." He's simply saying, earth is not our home. We are foreign products moving toward our eternal home. As we move toward home, God is closely inspecting us to see if there's any flaw before departure. It's your responsibility to be ready at the time of departure. Unfortunately, many will be left behind. However, you cannot blame anyone but yourself for your unpreparedness.

Many people wish they were never born for various reasons. Wait a minute! Stop thinking like that! You are special! You were chosen out of four million sperms to experience a journey called life. You're not here by accident. God is not haphazard. He doesn't make mistakes. Your life is not a fluke. God knew you before he formed you. You may not like the way your life has gone, but don't let your grievance take you to the grave. I will admit some things will make you grieve. But how you respond to what happens to you will either promote you or demote you. So if you want to be promoted, stop whining! Get off your pity pot and get ready for the many challenges you will encounter.

The scripture says we should give thanks not in some things but in everything; even when you are at your lowest. This is the time when you will experience growth spurts. Growth spurts are signs of strength. The Bible says our lives become brighter and more beautiful as God enters our lives, and as our lives reflect God's character, the more we bring him glory. You have to go low to grow. Even a seed has to go low before it can grow. You may not like your lowliness, but lowliness is the pathway to holiness.

As you move forward in life, you will be found with flaws. And as a result, people will talk negatively of you, not realizing we're all cut from the same cloth. They don't realize that what they do to you they do to themselves. The truth is, they don't want to face the truth about themselves; therefore, they waste valuable time talking negatively and criticizing everyone else. The fear of what they might discover if they honestly face the defects in their characters will keep them living in the prison of denial. Only when God shows us the truth about our faults and failures can we begin to work on them. That's when you will begin to see or experience *evolution*.

It's Evolution

Evolution is the process of changing formation; it is the process of a continual change from a lower state to a higher and more complex state or condition.

Everyone that comes into this world will experience the process of evolution. You cannot stop this process no matter how hard you try. We are evolving from birth to the time of our departure from earth. For nine months, you were evolving in your mother's womb. However, the process is not over. The fun has just begun. Life is not only a journey but a responsibility. Now that you're here, you have a contribution to make to the world that only you can make. Only you can be you and do what you are assigned to do. There is no duplication of you. God has uniquely designed each of us with special gifts and talents to serve to the world. All your talents and abilities come from God and should be used for his glory. It doesn't matter if you are a preacher, a teacher, a fireman, a farmer, a fisherman, a scientist, a zoologist, a biologist, a pathologist, an optometrist, or an archaeologist; everything came from God and should be used for his glory. Which one are you? Hold that thought!

The Bible says there are different abilities to perform service, but the same God-given abilities to all for the particular service (1 Corinthians 12:6 TEV).

You are the only one that can do what you have been assigned to do. No one can play your role. Regardless how you look or how old you are, it is inexcusable not to use the gifts and abilities that God has given you.

What you are is God's gift to you; what you do with yourself is your gift to God. (Danish proverb)

Tragically, many people have misused and abused their gifts for selfish reasons. God wants you to use what he has given you for his glory and not for selfish gain. To abuse and misuse what was given to you is symbolic to a lack of appreciation. God deserves your best and nothing less. Bringing God glory is another one of our responsibilities. Some people have tried to steal God's glory. They want all the glory for themselves. We have been commanded to reflect and live for his glory, not to steal it. You could go to prison for that. Since God created all things, he deserves all the glory. The Bible says, "You are worthy, O Lord our God, to receive glory and honor and praise. For you created everything" (Revelation 4:11 NLT).

When everything in creation fulfills its purpose, it brings glory to God, including the birds and the bees, the flowers and the trees. Refusing to bring God glory is prideful rebellion, which is also what caused Satan to be shot out of heaven faster than a frog can flick a fly. This is not your role. You must find out what your role is and fulfill it. That's right. If you're not sure about your role, ask yourself, "What am I good at doing? What are my special talents and abilities?" There's your answer. It's ludicrous to be trying to do something that will have you looking like a fool. If God didn't give you the gift or the ability to hold a tune from the womb, leave it to the ones who can. Some people can't hold a tune in a bucket. If it's not your gift, put it back in the bag!

The laws of the universe function under the principles of evolution. God has designed man and all his creation to undergo various stages of evolution. Here's an example: Like a tree, we must go through opposition and much criticism in order to bear new fruit. But to avoid opposition and criticism means to be average. As a tree grows, the bark stretches. As it stretches and splits, new layers begin to grow. As the seasons change, the tree goes through changes such as enduring the bitter cold in the winter. In the fall, the leaves take on beautiful colors and fall to the ground. Colors are light energy. Colors influence our emotions, our health, and our thoughts. Color reminds us that the season of change is in full effect. Like the changes that occur in nature, it must also occur in man.

Have anyone ever told you that you don't look like you used to? What happened? That's because you are evolving. At birth, you may have been as pretty as a picture; but now, fifteen years later, the prettiness has left the picture. One, two, *look* at you! What are you going to do?

Be Humble

Humility comes from the Latin word *humus*, which means earth. Earth is a low place. Humility is getting down to earth; it means freedom from arrogance that grows out of the recognition that all we have comes from God alone. It has nothing to do with belittling yourself but exalting and praising others, especially God. It's not thinking less of yourself but thinking of yourself less.

True humility has nothing to do with pride, but gratitude, since God is both our creator and redeemer, our existence and what we need depends on him (John 15:5).

Humility always acts in your favor. It doesn't weaken you; it strengthens you. When you humble yourself before God, he will lead you to the doors of greatness. The world defines greatness in terms of power, possessions, and prestige. In a world filled with arrogance, humility can barely be seen. However, Jesus measured it in terms of service to others, not self-serving status. God measures our greatness by the number of people you serve, not by how many serve you.

Humble people will not call all the attention to themselves like some people I know. Some people love attention. I'm not talking about the attention you should be getting from your spouse but the kind that thinks the world revolves around them. Nothing blocks progress like arrogance. A lot of our service is self-serving. We serve to get attention, promotion, recognition, and advancement. However, you will not find humble people living in the limelight of life. In fact, they are busy trying to avoid it. They are quite satisfied by quietly serving in the shadows.

By nature, we were born selfish creatures, and that is why serving others is opposing. We are confronted with the opportunity to serve others daily. But if you really want to please God and live a more fulfilling life, you must be willing and ready to do what seems strange and insane to others and the rest of the world. You must be willing to give when others hate, to help when everyone else is passing by. Christianity is not a religion but a lifestyle, and the heart of that lifestyle is about preferring others. What are you doing? I've seen some people spend their whole life doing nothing. That's insane! They want to sit under a sycamore and sip on chardonnay all day. You were created to serve, not sit. Complacency is evidence of spiritual laziness.

You must understand that humility is an important part of life. Today, people are more concerned about social status rather than social service.

Practice Self-Discipline

The principle of self-discipline is essential for life. Self-discipline is regulating one's self for the sake of self-improvement. When you're busy regulating your own affairs, you don't have time to regulate someone else's. That's right. When you are busy regulating and trying to improve yourself, you discover more things about yourself. There are some people who know more about everybody else's life than they do their own. Why is that? It's because they lack self-discipline. You cannot see yourself when your attention is set on everyone else.

In this life, a disciplined life is very essential. An undisciplined life is like a ship without a sail. An undisciplined life is like a fish out of water that's soon to die. An undisciplined life is like a ship without a rudder. An undisciplined life is like living in a land without laws. An undisciplined life goes wherever the wind blows. That's right.

If you have a child who's always out of control and have no respect for their elders, it is because they lack discipline. Discipline is twofold:

1. Negative side, which is correction and punishment
2. Positive side, which is instruction and training

If you refuse to follow instruction, which is the positive side, you will be corrected from a positive point of view.

Sometimes God allows things to happen to us to make us better. Discipline is a sign of love. The purpose of self-discipline is to avoid self-destruction. An undisciplined life is headed for self-destruction. To avoid self-destruction, follow God's instructions. They will keep you from going over the edge. Everyone's life is driven by something, whether it's painful memories, doubt, fear, drugs, sex, alcoholism, money, materialism, unforgiveness, or need for approval.

Webster defines the word *drive* as "to guide, to control, or to direct." What's the driving force in your life? There are many other forces that can drive you over the edge, but don't go over the edge. A well-disciplined life keeps you from going over the edge.

Self-discipline is a must for those who want to improve their lives instead of destroying it. Every military branch teaches a version of this life-changing method.

Many people are not interested in self-discipline. They choose to engage in things that satisfy their short-term needs at the expense of long-term failure. So beware of what failures do and avoid what they do and do what they don't do because oftentimes, it's what they don't do that makes them a failure.

God requires that we live a self-disciplined life, whether we want to or not. An undisciplined life is a life that refuses to surrender.

Be Willing to Surrender

Surrender means to yield or give oneself up to the power and control of another. Surrendering is sacrificing your life, time, and attention in order to change what needs to be changed in your life. God is saying, "I want to be the center of your attention." Instead, we give our time and attention to a lot of negative things that keep us in bondage. I don't know about you, but I despise living in bondage. Whatever you are not in control of is controlling you. That's bondage. However, God is not going to hold you at gunpoint, slap slob from your mouth, and say, "Stick 'em up!" God is love, not cruelty. However, he does have his own way of getting your attention. The principle of surrender is essential for change. To experience change, you must surrender to change. Many people are bound because they want to be bound. A person living in bondage cannot live a satisfying and fulfilling life that God intended. King Solomon, a very wise man, said, "An untimely birth is better than an unsatisfied life" (Ecclesiastes 6:3).

I have seen wealthy people pretending to be happy and fulfilled only to discover they are not. They make six-figure salaries, drive expensive cars, live in fine houses and well-groomed communities, and take expensive vacations. However, behind all that disguise, the families are shattered, their marriage is on the rocks, their children are hooked on dope and alcohol and living in depression. When you are living in this kind of bondage, life is beating up on you. Christ came to give us the abundant life, not a life in bondage. Whom the Son makes free is free indeed. A man's effort for obtaining satisfaction that falls short often causes frustration. A satisfied life is a gift from God, and man shall be motivated by the brevity of his own life to experience it to the fullest. Are you full?

Paul asked a question, "Shall we continue in bondage because we are not under the law, but under grace? God forbid!" (Roman 6:15 NKJV).

If you get caught committing a crime, the first thing the officer tells you to do is to put your hands up or lay prostrate, which is an act of surrendering. However, if you resist or fight back, you could be shot or killed. Surrender is an act of your own will; you have the freedom to do whatever you want to do, but consequences will follow. What would you do? Make the wrong move—your life could end.

Surrendering is not an easy task. In fact, it is an intense perpetual warfare against your self-centered nature. If you do not surrender your life, time, and attention to God, you will eventually surrender it to something or someone else. Whether it's pride, self, lust, money, resentment, prestige, power, possessions, materialism, doubt, fear, or another individual. What have you surrendered to? It is in our weakness that we experience God's strength. We must rely on him for effectiveness rather than our own strength, power, effort, or talent.

It was William Booth, founder of the Salvation Army, who said, "The greatness of man's power is found in the measure of his surrender." Hmm.

You know when you have surrendered to God when you trust him to work things out when you can't see a way out. You don't have to always be in charge. Trust is a true sign of a fully surrendered life. When God told him to get out of his country, Father Abraham trusted God's leading without knowing where he was taking him. However, I believe one of the most difficult areas of a surrendered life for many people is found in the area of their finances. Don't get me wrong. I believe God wants you wealthy, but he doesn't want you to allow your possessions to possess you. That's when you've gone too far. The most valuable things in life are not your valuables, but your values (Luke 12:15).

More people have allowed money to replace God in their lives than you can imagine. Acquiring wealth is not a sin, but failing to use it for God's glory is. Many people have a bad habit of doing this. That's why Jesus talked and taught more about money and how it should be used more than heaven or hell. How you manage money determines how God can bless and manage you. What's in your wallet?

Surrendering is not just a once-in-a-lifetime act. Paul said, "I die daily." We must practice dying daily to our self-centered nature. Surrendering is a perpetual, ongoing, lifelong event.

People who refuse to surrender their lives for something better are selfish, self-centered, edgy, egotistic people who have failed to realize that the world does not revolve around them, neither did they create it. Peace is a gift from God. If you never surrender to him, you will never experience true peace. That's a point to ponder.

The Transforming Power of Forgiveness

In Hebrew *forgiveness* means to "send off," not go off. When God forgives us, he sends our sins off. Never to be remembered anymore (Hebrews 10:17). Forgiveness is a very important part of our lives.

I have discovered in this life people will go off on you, disappoint you, which leads to disappointments. They will lie to you, misuse you, and abuse you, whether it's advertently or inadvertently. If you truly want to live, learn how to forgive. Because when you fail to forgive, you hold yourself hostage. Imagine holding yourself at gunpoint. When people hold themselves at gunpoint, it looks as though they are threatening to commit suicide. When you fail to forgive people of their offenses, you are threatening suicide. Wait a minute! Hold that trigger! Let's talk about this.

Forgiveness is a choice. It is an act of restoration and reconciliation. When you forgive, you are restored back from death to life, and you are reconciled back to God. I believe forgiveness is an act of love. God is love. Since God is love, who are you? You should be a version of who God is. There's too much hate in the world. Some say there's a thin line between love and hate. For many people, love has become one of the things people love to hate. Life is all about love, not hate. Love should be your greatest aim and your primary objective. What are you aiming for? Love or hate? You cannot walk with God and hold hands with hate.

If you continue to hold hands with hate, love will continue to bypass your temple, and as a result, you will continue to hate. When you harbor hate in your heart, you will become hateful. What are you harboring in your heart? Your willingness to forgive qualifies you to walk with God.

Inside resentment, you will find the word *resent*, which means to "send over again." When resentment is in control, your situation will continue to repeat itself over and over again. That's why it is important for us to deal with ourselves before we deal with someone else. When you harbor hate in your heart, it will manifest itself in the eyes of others by casting a dark shadow because it's evil.

If you harbor resentment in your heart, it will virtually kill you. Not only will it kill you, but it will also kill your joy and your peace of mind and will have you plotting revenge. Wait a minute! Vengeance is not yours! Put it back! You could get locked down for that. Hate and resentment are two thieves you don't need in your temple because they will rob you of contentment.

Resentment, which is contentment turned upside down, will make you sick. The first thing that will get sick is the mind because there's no peace. When there's no peace, a palace made of pearls will look polluted in the eyes of the beholder. Stop making yourself sick. You can be healed when you forgive.

Many people refuse to forgive. They would rather see the guilty party get hit in the head with a hammer or struck by a train or fall from an airplane or fall into a spewing hot volcano. Wait a minute! That's not love! Always remember this, there will come a time when you will need someone to forgive you. What will you do when they refuse to forgive you? Hold that thought! Don't reach for the hammer! It's not *hammer time*.

God wants you to value relationships and make an effort to resolve them whenever there's a rift or conflict. It doesn't matter if you are the offender or the offended; God expects you to make the first move. In fact, the stronger person will always take the initiative. Don't wait for the other party to make the move. The other party may have their mind set on partying. That's right. In previous conflicts, many people act as though they did nothing at all. Wow! Playing innocent is not the answer.

Here's something else you need to know, especially if you're married and your marriage is on the rocks: unforgiveness will lead your marriage to prison. Wait a minute! Prison is for pimps!

Move Beyond Your Past

Some people just cannot get past their past. What's in your past that you cannot get past. If you cannot get past your past, your future will pass you by. Your past contains a list of things that can hold you captive. If you want to move into your future, turn loose your past and leave it in the past. The only time you should be going back into your past is to pick up a life lesson. Our past is full of life's lessons—some good, some bad. If you take a journey back into your past to pick up more than a life lesson, you will become entangled with the *ghost of the past*. The ghost of the past will have you grieving greatly because you picked up a piece of your past that was poisoned. It is a dangerous thing to pick up poisoned pieces from your past.

One of the most destructive things you can do is to be bound and shackled to your past. Life is too short to allow yourself to be a prison inmate of past mistakes and bad choices. The prison of previous mistakes comes with guilt and regrets. Today they can lead you captive, torturing you with images of what you could have done or been. People like this become their own warden, prolonging the sentence. In fact, they are the judge, jury, and prosecuting attorney, giving themselves a life sentence of misery and regrets. Stop prosecuting yourself! Get off that regret trip! Come out of your past! If you don't, you could die there. Nothing blocks progress like someone who can't get beyond their past. When I looked into my past, I saw that it was all a setup. Your life and my life have been predestined. That's right. You are a spiritual being on a spiritual journey. How you respond to what happens to you on this journey will either promote you or demote you. You cannot understand where you are going until you understand where you have been. Where have you been? Wait a minute! Hold that thought! God knew you before he formed you in your mother's womb (Jeremiah 1:5).

How can God know you before he formed you, unless you preexisted before formed? Have you ever had a déjà vu? A déjà vu, unlike a rendezvous, is a mesmerizing moment. I remember having a déjà vu in the middle of a college football game. That's when I thought I was literally losing my mind. Later on I discovered it was just a déjà vu. A déjà vu is a French word for seeing something you seemingly have seen before. In other words, it was just an illusion. Could it mean I have been here before?

Regardless of all the tragedies and difficulties that have occurred in your life, it was all a setup. However, you should not spend years or a lifetime of regrets in the graveyard of guilt, dealing with the corpse of the past. What is your past dictating to you?

Part Two

Renewing Your Mind

Renewing Your Mind

Getting rid of the old and bringing in the new will actually transform you. Everything began with a thought. To change your life is no exception. Behind every act lies a thought. Whatever thoughts you are thinking will show up at your door to serve you. Planting a thought is like planting a seed. Every thought you plant will produce an act or behavior.

The Bible says, "Don't be conformed to this world but be transformed by renewing your mind" (Romans12:2).

Your life is shaped by the way you think. If where you are is not where you want to be, you must change the way you think. If you don't like where you live, change your address. The Supreme Court says you can live wherever you want to live.

You must train your mind to think in a different way about everything. Every time your mind becomes renewed in an area, you are being birthed into a new awareness. When you are struggling with something, it means your mind needs to be renewed in that area. Mind renewal will cause you to be rebuilt, restored, reconditioned, reprogrammed, and reconstructed. Some people may say negative things about you, but your responses to what people say and life circumstances will determine your personal outcome. How you respond to your outcome will determine your personal income.

There are two things that will always motivate you. Those two things are pain and pleasure. Pain and pleasure come from the same source—one is night, the other is morning. You need them both because together they make a day (Genesis1:5).

The Bible says weeping may endure for a night, but joy comes in the morning. Your morning signifies pleasure. Pain and pleasure are master motivators. Do not view them as negative things. Pain is an indication that you need to make some adjustments somewhere. Usually, that place is in the area of your consciousness. When people make mistake after mistake, it is no longer called a mistake but a misperception. Changing the way you think is like a cool, refreshing drink. But you should never feed your mind anything that you don't want to experience because your experiences are simply the results of your inner thoughts.

It's All in Your Mind

What is checking in at the port of your consciousness? Is it good or is it bad? Is it true or is it a lie? Whatever is checking in and out of your consciousness are the results of your experiences. Where your attention goes, your power flows. Where is your power flowing? This is why you have to edit your thoughts daily.

Believe it or not, every day you are creating your own reality show by allowing whatever is checking in and out of your consciousness. Thoughts are everything. If you don't like what's showing up at your show, you have the authority to shut it down because you are the writer, the producer, the director, and the CEO of your own show. Your God-given power of the mind flows into whatever has your attention, thus creating your own reality show. What's showing up at your show? What's showing up in the theater of your mind? Your mind is like a camera. Whatever you focus on and allow to be taken will be your reward. Whatever goes in and out has to first come through you. You control what goes in and out.

News flash! Inside your mind, you will find something called quality control. Quality control is where you should be in control to filter out the bad from the good. Quality control determines your quality of life. Everything and everybody that shows up in your life are the results of your inner thoughts. Thoughts have magnetic power. Your outer world of circumstances is shaped by your inner world of thoughts. Who willed your world?

Had not God used his mind to create the world, there would not be a world. He used his mind to create the flowers, the trees, the oceans, and the seas. He used his awesome mind to create the intricate design of the human mind. If you're not happy about the world you are in, think again. Everything begins with a thought; your mind is your most powerful asset.

Many people are unhappy about a lot of things in their lives. Many are unhappy about their relationships. Many are unhappy about their financial statuses. Many are unhappy about where they live. Many are unhappy about the way they look. Many are unhappy about their careers. Many are unhappy about whom—or should I say what—they married. If you are unhappy about something in your life, you don't have to pray to God to change it.

God is waiting for you to make a move. He's waiting on you to think a thought that will change your world. If you want something you never had before, you must do something you've never done before. And keep in mind that whatever state you are in, you put yourself there. There's always a corresponding thought that goes along with an action that is tied to the situation that you find yourself in. If you have a car that you have to push up and down the road, don't get mad and shoot the car. Get one you can drive around. If you shoot it, people may think you have lost your mind.

There are a lot of things that go on inside our heads, including dreams and things. There is nothing you can do about a déjà vu. If you focus on something or someone long enough, you will eventually dream about it. Dreams are a series of thoughts that appear to you in mental images. Your mind is also like a television screen when it comes to dreams. Some dreams are riveting while others are frightening. Some people wish that they could change the channel because of the scene they see in their dreams. It's all in your head.

Dreams are said to be the mind's way of making sense of various issues that it deals with in any given time—be it work, time of trouble, family, or relationships. Dreams help sort out all the information and events that are inputted during waking hours, creating a way for a person to understand what is going on inside their head, to solve problems, to gain clarity and insight on situations and issues. It is God's way of communicating with men (Numbers 12:6).

You should pay attention to what's going on inside your head because something or somebody is trying to tell you something. Some thoughts serve as a premonitions. Not every thought that comes dancing through your head is a warning of your demise. Thoughts can have either positive or negative impact on your life.

Do you not know that you can think you're going to die and eventually you will die? Just because you have a pain does not mean it's the end of your journey. Pain is just an indication of an abnormality. Sometimes you may have to use your will to live.

Inside your head, you have what is called a will. It is a very powerful principle. You can use your willpower to live when the doctor has declared you're going to die. Because of your will to live, you are still alive. Willpower is located in your forehead, and next to it is the power of understanding. The power of understanding goes into the depth of your being. Understanding goes into the intuitive power, which is God centered. Willpower, along with the power of understanding, is expressed in the words, "Not my will, but Thy will be done." This is not a negative statement. It is God's will that you be healed and in good health and prosperous (3 John 2).

Thoughts can heal, but they can also kill. There's no secret about that. There's a lot of thing s that goes on inside our heads.

Earl Nightingale discovered what he called the strangest secret: you will become what you think about. Hmm, think about that.

Every secret will remain a secret until the secret is revealed. You become what you love is no longer a secret because that secret had been revealed.

There's a lot that goes on inside our minds. You may even think from time to time that you're losing your mind. However, that could be a good thing.

Have You Lost Your Mind?

If you have not lost your mind, now will be a good time. It's OK for you to act like you have lost your mind if you have the mind of Christ. Have you lost your mind? Hold up! Wait a minute! The Bible says, "Let this mind be in you which was in Christ Jesus" (Philippians 2:5).

This simply means once you get the mind of Christ, hold on to it. It means keep thinking this, that is, constantly maintain this attitude within yourself as long as you live. This is called the principle of replacement. If you don't have the mind of Christ, your mind is currently in a crisis. Your mind is conformed to the mind of Christ as you constantly spend time with Christ. Spending time with Christ means becoming more like Christ.

People need more than bread for their lives. They must feed on every word of God (Matthew 4:4).

The truth will transform you. Spiritual truth and spiritual growth is the process of replacing lies with the truth. Jesus prayed, "Sanctify them by the truth, your word is true." Daily Bible reading will keep you in range of God's voice. No other habits can transform your life and make you more like Christ than daily reflection on God's word. A mind is a terrible thing to waste. An intimate relationship with Christ comes only from spending time in his presence and applying his principles.

What you put into your mind determines what comes out in words, deeds, and actions. Paul taught us to reprogram our minds with thoughts that are true, pure, noble, lovely, excellent, and praiseworthy. Take note on what you are putting in your mind through television, movies, and magazines. Does your mind like to wander? Your mind is too small to be wandering alone. Inquiring minds like to roam; even when your mind should be at home, it's somewhere roaming in Rome. A roaming mind will have you serving time like a criminal. Your mind cannot be trusted; it will get you busted. Sometimes we do things we know we shouldn't do, but we do them anyway and expect to get away. Instead of getting away, we get busted. That's why your mind cannot be trusted.

Ladies, if you have a man who has a habit of beating you, don't kill him. All you got to do is just act like you have lost your mind, and that problem will be solved. God doesn't want us to be fools. However, there comes a time when you have to play it cool and a time when you have to act like a fool, especially when someone is breaking the rule.

Every Thought Yields Something of Its Kind

Think a thought; reap an act. Your thought has a magnetic power. Your thoughts will either benefit you or deprave and deprive you. Behind everything you do is a thought.

You must see your thoughts as seeds and our orderly, harmonious, systematic universe as the soil in which those seeds are sown.

The farmer that sowed seed in his field cannot resist the pull of gravity nor the process of germination.

Just like the farmer, you cannot ignore the harvest nature of reality. In fact, you are always sowing some kind of crop. All your thoughts will produce a result of the same kind. Thoughts are like a pendulum that swings outward as the thoughts take shape in your mind and project outward, then swing back to you with the same kind of energy you used to project it.

Just as the law guarantees that each thought will produce a harvest, it also guarantees that nothing comes without a price.

The cosmos must remain in balance. What you desire must be paid with something of equal value. You must always give up something in order to gain something. And you will usually know what it is. It's whatever that blocks you from depending entirely on God for your means of support and succor. In this equation of personal and universal economy, like attracts like. You must understand and live by this principle if you are to benefit from it and live in harmony in God's system.

What you project into the mental plane whether it is thought, faith, declaration, or a gift to another will return to you in the same form. Gifts will produce gifts. Sorrow will produce sorrow. Wealth will produce wealth. Science reflects the same concept of law of thermodynamics. This law says energy may never be created or destroyed; it can only be changed. You are energy. You were created to last forever. Thoughts are energy in motion. What you think will manifest in the same manner. So be careful how you think; your life is shaped by your thoughts. The Bible warns us to watch what we think and how we think. Because we have angels around us to guard us and to reward us according to the way we think and what we say (Psalms 91:11).

What You Say

From the abundance of the heart, the mouth speaks. Even the words you speak begin with a thought. It all starts in the mind. Your thoughts need to be carefully edited on a daily basis. If not, you can easily find yourself saying the wrong thing. Some people say whatever comes into their minds. Hold up! Wait a minute! You should put some caution to it.

Remember the old saying, "Loose lips sink ships." That means if you're not careful, you can say something that will take you under. You can easily end up in a place you don't want to be, asking yourself, "How did I get here?" I'll tell you how. You let your mouth take you there. Words of advice, if you don't know what to say, don't say anything at all.

Researchers have concluded that speaking wholesome words and thinking wholesome thoughts can actually change a person's DNA. Wow! Words are powerful. We speak them every day. Sticks and stones may break my bones, but words can kill. Who have you been killing with your words? Wait a minute! Do you not know that you can be hanged by your own tongue? Stop hanging yourself! Life and death lies within the power of your words (Proverbs 18:21).

You're tongue cannot be tamed, but your tongue can tame you. If you do not want to experience the hot seat, be careful what you say because your words can take you there. Where are your words taking you? Where is your mouth leading you?

I have discovered that there are approximately thirty different types of tongues. Here they are: the *lying* tongue, the *flattering* tongue, the *manipulating* tongue, the *divisive* tongue, the *argumentative* tongue, the *boasting* tongue, the *self-depreciating* tongue, the *gossiping* tongue, the *defraying* tongue, the *belittling* tongue, the *cynical* tongue, the *know-it-all* tongue, the *harsh* tongue, the *tactful* tongue, the *intimidating* tongue, the *rude* tongue, the *judgmental* tongue, the *self-absorbed* tongue, the *cursing* tongue, the *discouraging* tongue, the *doubting-Thomas* tongue, the *indiscreet* tongue, and the *silent* tongue. Which tongue are you?

You have a variety of tongues to choose from. The Bible says, "The tongue of the righteous bring forth wisdom, but a perverse tongue will be cut out" (Proverb 10:31). It is self-explanatory. A perverse tongue is the gateway to misery. Can you imagine being without a tongue?

You have to be careful in what you say because your words have a direct impact on your life. The good that you experience is the result of your choice of words. Your words create your environment, whether you like the environment or not. Therefore, you must make sure that you are not creating something you don't want. Because what you say is what you get. That's the way the cookie crumbles and how the water falls.

Remember, "loose lips sink ships." Before you go shooting off at the mouth, check to see what is about to flow from the tip of your tongue because it will manifest itself in your experiences and will show up at your door to teach you a lesson. Your words frame your world. The words of other people cannot frame your world unless you accept them. What you say can change your DNA. You have a variety of tongues to choose from. However, if you choose the wrong tongue, you can be hanged.

Be careful what you think in secret because those thoughts will eventually be revealed. What you think in secret will be brought to the light. Every thought you have, whether you speak them verbally or not, shall be brought to the light. If you do not express your emotion, your body language will tell what you are thinking. Your body language speaks volumes, such as the way you stand, the way you sit, your facial expression, the way you walk, and the way you fold your arms. You can tell when someone has an attitude by the way he or she storms out of a room. Perhaps they are experiencing the quiet storm.

Trouble in My Mind

Are you troubled in your mind? Trouble can get in your mind whereby you have to cry sometimes. There's an old song entitled "Trouble in My Way." Trouble can be a good thing. That's right. In this life, trouble comes and trouble goes.

God uses troubles and difficult circumstances to develop our character. Your tribulation is the gateway to your transformation. When trouble comes knocking at your door, try not to ask, "Why me?" Why not you? You were chosen, just like everyone else, out of four hundred million sperms to stand toe-to-toe with trouble. Trouble doesn't come to destroy you but to transform you. Trouble has been assigned to you. Trouble has your name on it, and there's nothing you can do about it. Wherever you go, trouble goes. You can run, but you cannot hide. So get used to it, friend. Trouble will be here until the end. Whenever you are in trouble, you are in the perfect position to experience God's awesome power of deliverance. He uses trouble to draw us closer to himself. Had it not been for trouble, many of us would be in a lot of trouble. The right kind of trouble will have you running for cover. No one makes propositions for oppositions. Oppositions are used for transitions. God uses oppositions to transform us. You cannot hide from them. No matter where you go, trouble will find you. You can climb the highest mountain to escape trouble, but trouble will find you and greet you with a Coke and a smile. Knock, knock. Who's there? Trouble! Trouble who? Troublemaker. In everyone's life, some rain must fall.

Everything that happens to you has spiritual significance, whether you like it or not. Romans 8:28 sheds the light: We know that all things work together for the good of those who love God and are called according to his purpose.

There is a grand designer behind the scene, controlling everything. In fact, God's plans for your life involve all that happens to you, including your trouble, your pain, your disappointments, your afflictions, sickness, and oppositions. We are like jewels being shaped with a chisel by the Master's hand. Like a potter forming a vessel on the wheel. God is shaping you into a benchmark of something beautiful. In fact, God has always been in the business of forming and filling. He will take care of the filling if you can withstand the forming. The forming must always precede the filling.

Here's an example: When he formed man, he filled him with his Spirit. When he formed the earth, he filled it with creeping creatures, beasts of the field, oceans and seas, flowers and trees. When he formed the heavens, he filled it with angels. When he formed the clouds, he filled it with the process of osmosis. When he formed the temple, he filled it with his Shechinah glory, which is the invisible manifestation of his presence.

The potter does not form a vessel without having something to fill it. Like the potter, God is behind the wheel, forming and shaping you into something greater and more beautiful. And whatever he has declared you to be, you shall be it. And remember, an unlearned lesson is guaranteed to repeat itself until you get it right. If you never get it right, that lesson will haunt you like an unwelcomed group of animated gargoyles eagerly waiting to pounce on you.

Part Three

Defeating Temptation

> Happy is the man who do not give in and do wrong when he is
> tempted. For afterwards he will get as his reward a crown of life
> that God has promised those who love him. (James 1:12 LB)

Martin Luther wrote, "My temptation has been my master in divinity."

To be tempted is to be tested. Life is filled with tests. As long as your body is breathing, you're going to be tested. However, if you stumble and fail a test, it is not the end of your journey. If for some reason you fall, instead of giving up, keep looking up! Temptation may be Satan's primary way to wipe you out. However, it is God's way of testing you. That's right! God uses it to test your level in life and to develop your character. Just like in school, you will be tested to determine if you qualify for the next level. If you fail, God will not send you to hell. However, you should turn to him for help. Heaven has a twenty-four-hour emergency hotline available to the whole world. If you never request help, help will bypass your temple. Since God is standing by, waiting to help you, destroy that yoke in your yard. Why do you keep wrestling with it?

The Bible declares if we cry out for help, help will come to our rescue. God knows and understands our weaknesses for he faced all the same temptation or test we do, yet he did not give in to sin (Hebrews 4:15 NLT).

Temptation can become a building block rather than a stumbling block once you realize that it is as much of an occasion to do right as it is to do wrong. In fact, it is an invitation to a life lesson. The Bible says, "Happy is the man who do not give in to temptation." Another scripture says, "My brother count it all joy when you fall into divers temptation" (James 1:2 NKJV).

These experiences are to be accepted with great joy, not for the sake of the test itself, but because of the positive work God can accomplish through the testing.

Happiness is much more than a feeling. It is a state of good fortune, well-being, and contentment. Every time you turn your back on temptation, you move closer toward a life of good fortune, joy, and contentment. Wait a minute! Does life get any better that this?

You may have a strong faith, but you also have weak spots. And that's where temptation usually strikes. It doesn't matter if you're the president or a hero living in the same residence, you are going to be tempted. That's why you should strengthen and protect your weak areas because a chain is only as strong as its weakest link. That's just how the cookie crumbles.

How Temptation Works

Temp means temperature. When you are really being tempted, your body temperature rises and your heart starts pounding and your desire or appetite increases. What in the world is going on? Well, that's the way we've been wired by our Creator. You have what is called a normal desire, such as a desire to be loved and cared for, and you have evil desires, which the devil uses to get you to give in to temptation. In fact, he has used the same strategy since the beginning of Creation. Every temptation basically follows the same pattern.

Martin Luther once said, "There are three things that make a Christian—prayer, meditation, and temptation." Luther may have great difficulty getting anyone to agree with him. If, indeed, temptation is a sort of necessary evil, one would be hard pressed to find a non-Christian who would call it evil or a Christian who would find it necessary.

A careful look at the scriptures will prove Luther right. Temptation plays a vital role in the growth and maturing of the Christian. And what is more, temptation played a significant role in the preparation of Jesus Christ for his public presentation as Israel's Messiah. In the wilderness, our Lord's fitness for such a mission is tested. In the temptation, Satan never assails the identification of Christ as Israel's Messiah. He simply tries to divert his attention from his task.

Satan's first line of attack came through hunger, which our Lord experienced due to his forty-day fast. Satan's suggestions were based on several erroneous premises. First, a God who is good would not deprive one of his creatures. Going without food cannot be the will of God. Such was the insinuation in the temptation of the first Adam in the garden. "Surely a good God would not withhold such a good thing as this fruit," Satan suggested. Second, Satan supposes that men serve God and submit to his will because God bribes them to do so with material blessings. Remember Satan's statement to God concerning Job: "Then Satan answered the Lord, 'Does Job fear God for nothing?'" (Job 1:9). Satan could not conceive Jesus submitting to the will of the Father when it meant personal discomfort. If personal pleasure comes before God's will, our Lord would never have gone to the cross of Calvary. If submission and obedience did not involve personal sacrifice, the atonement would never have been accomplished. This would have been the potential outcome had our Lord followed Satan's advice.

Satan's schemes are predictable. That's why Paul said, "We are not ignorant of his devices" (2 Corinthians 2:11). Surprised? When people are surprised, you can see it in their eyes.

Here are four steps:

Step 1 is desire. Satan tries to identify a lustful *desire* inside you. It may be a desire to steal or kill. It may even be an appetite or a normal desire like the desire to feel pleasure. One of the greatest gifts God has given us is the ability to enjoy pleasure. However, the devil will use it against you. He will use whatever means necessary to get you trapped or entangled in his web of deceit. He works on your internal desire. If there was no desire, it's no longer temptation but contemplation. It has to be something that has the ability or the power to draw or seduce to do wrong.

Step 2 is doubt. If God said it, believe it. If the devil said it, don't believe it. His primary objective is to get you to doubt God and everything he has declared. Doubt is when you allow your opinion to interfere with your decision making. Doubt is simply not believing or unbelief in God and his provisions. While unbelief does not hinder God's faithfulness, it does affect your capacity to receive the benefits of that faithfulness. When doubt is in control, what God has said becomes questionable.

Beware of the temptation that often comes with doubt. If you are dealing with bouts of doubt, realize that you are especially vulnerable to temptation. Even as you search for answers, protect yourself by meditating on the unshakable, infallible principles of God. Whenever there's bouts of doubt, temptation can easily knock you out.

Step 3 is deception. The devil is the master of deception, which is nothing more than trickery or the act of deceiving. Who's fooling who? Who's lying to whom?

Satan is incapable of telling the truth, and that's why he's called the father of lies. Once you realize that the devil is in your ears whispering sweet lies, don't believe anything he says. When the devil comes knocking on your door, ask, "Who is it?" If it's the devil, tell him to go away, not today. If you give him an inch, he'll come in and crack your chain and take over the whole house. Satan is not some fairy-tale imaginary being. He is very real and ruthless. The more you know about your enemy, the greater your chances become to defeat him.

Step 4 is disobedience. Obedience is a positive, active response to what a person hears. Disobedience is just the opposite.

The first and most crucial act of disobedience occurred in the Garden of Eden where Adam and Eve ate the forbidden fruit (Genesis 3). Once he got their attention, he stole their residence. They had it made in the shade, but the devil was able to lure them out of the shade. He lured them from a garden of paradise to a garden of garbage and laughed about it. I believe one of the best ways to defeat temptation is to divert your attention. Even Satan knows this to be true because he used it against Jesus. Where your attention goes, your power flows. When you play with temptation, you are setting yourself up for failure. That's right. It's best not to toll with temptation. It is simply an invitation to a world of frustration and aggravation. Here's what you can do when temptation presents you with an invitation.

Divert Your Attention

You can't defeat temptation by fighting the feeling. Ignoring the temptation is far more effective than fighting it. Since temptation begins with a thought, the best way to arrest that thought is to divert that thought.

That's right. Don't fight it; turn from it. Stop giving your attention away. The battle is either won or lost in the vicinity of your mind where decisions are made.

Temptation begins by capturing your attention. Whatever gets your attention stimulates your emotions, and your emotions activate your behavior. Once your mind is tuned in to something different, the temptation loses its power. When temptation comes calling you on the phone, the best thing to do is to ignore it. Don't flirt with it. When we flirt with the temptation of the world, God calls it spiritual adultery. Your cheating heart is cheating on God as a believer and born-again Christian. The church is the bride of Christ (Revelation 19:7). But when you flirt with the temptation of the world, you are cheating on the groom. Whatever gets your attention the most will get the most of you. Some things just aren't worth it. The battle is either won or lost in the vicinity of your mind. Temptation is simply an invitation to misery, which explains why so many people are incarcerated. Misery loves company.

Recognize Your Pattern

It's not always the devil working behind the scene. If you fail to recognize your pattern of temptation, the devil will step back and watch you make a fool of yourself. Here's a parable of a man who went fishing and found a bed of hungry basses: As soon as his hook hit the water, he would hook another one. Ah yeah! He was hooking them faster than a frog can flick a fly. Suddenly, one fish said to the others, "Wait a minute! Wait a minute! Something fishy is going on! We're missing some members. Every time we're introduced to this tasty treat, one of us is snatched away. Mayday! Mayday! Pull away!" By the way, this is my made up parable.

If you never recognize what's going on, you will continue to be hooked by the same temptation. What are you hooked on? What are you feeding on? Whatever you don't feed will die.

There are some situations that you are more vulnerable to than others. Moreover, the devil knows exactly what kind of bait you're going to bite. As long as you continue to bite the bait he prepared for you, you will stay hooked. When a person is hooked on something, the price of freedom doesn't come free.

The Bible warns us to stay alert. "The devil is poised to pounce, and would like nothing better that to catch you napping" (1 Peter 5:8 MSG).

Ask yourself, "When am I most vulnerable? Is it when I am all alone in my home? Is it when I'm in a crowd of people? Who's with me when I'm most tempted? Is it when I'm around my friends? Neighbors? Coworkers?"

Once you recognize your pattern of temptation, prepare yourself to avoid it as much as possible. If you used to have a problem with booze, don't go around your boozing buddies. If you do, somebody is going to entice you to have a bud and a buzz.

Know where you are vulnerable. None of us is immune to temptation. It's easier to stay out of temptation than to get out of it. Why? If you give in to temptation, there are consequences. Temptation is a setup to be messed up.

Temptation is simply an invitation to a world of misery.

During Halloween, the children always go trick or treating. Sometimes, they get tricks instead of treats. The devil uses treats to trick people. Let the devil know what used to work doesn't work anymore. What used to depress you doesn't depress you anymore. What used to make you cry doesn't make you cry anymore. Tell that problem, "This is it! Enough is enough! I've had enough of your stuff. So put your tricks back in the bag! Silly rabbit tricks are for kids." Every time you defeat temptation, you gain more power over it, which causes you to get a little stronger each time. Never enter the ring thinking that you're going to win the fight without putting up a fight. That would be a foolish mistake. Never get overconfident when it comes to temptation. Don't be misled. Don't get tricked!

Jeremiah said, "The heart is desperately wicked. Who can know it?" (Jeremiah 17:9)

That means your mind will play tricks on you. Given the right circumstances, all of us are capable or subject to fall into sin. It doesn't matter who you are or who you think you are. What's good for the goose is also good for the gander.

The scripture says, don't be naïve and self-confident, you're not exempt. You could fall flat on your face as anyone else. Forget about self-confidence; it's useless. Cultivate God confidence (1 Corinthians 10:12 MSG).

Temptation is simply your invitation to a world of frustration, aggravation, and irritation. You may have the heart and the desire to do good or the right thing, but there's something about the lure and the power of sin and temptation and their ability to play with your weakness and frailty that leads you to your demise.

Temptation is like a thief lurking in the darkness, waiting for that perfect moment to strike. Some thieves will strip you of everything you have. You wake up only to discover all your goods are gone. Now you're looking bewildered, wondering what happened. Perhaps you were careless that night and left a window or a door unlocked. That's why it pays to be prepared for the unexpected.

That's why the Bible says "Be sober and vigilant, [which means "to keep watch" or "stay awake"] because your adversary the devil is like a roaring lion walking about, seeking whom he can mess up" (1 Peter 5:8 KJV). Another translation says, "Stay alert! The devil is poised to pounce, and would like nothing better than to catch you napping (1 Peter 5:8 MSG).

Satan is our adversary (opposer), but Jesus is our advocate (one who opposes our opposer). Satan's job is to accuse us before

God (Revelations 12:10). He's a ruthless prosecuting attorney in the heavenly courts. Christ and the Holy Spirit are our legal advocates, the defense attorneys, who help defend and plead our case before God day and night, providing a continual remedy for sin when we fall in or give in to it. That's something to shout about. It's quite obvious; Christ is our friend.

Grab a Friend

Not just any friend but a fruitful, faithful friend. No one succeeds alone. If you pray for help, God will send someone to shake you and wake you up to what's going on in your life. Some battles are baffling and will cause you to go ballistic. If you are losing the battle to a bad habit or an addiction and you're stuck in a repeated cycle of guilt, you will not succeed alone. Some temptations can only be conquered with the help of a praying partner who prays for you and encourages you. You can feed off each other's strength and wisdom.

The Bible says, "You are better off to have a friend than to be all alone . . . if you fall, your friend can help you up. But if you fall without a friend you are in trouble" (Ecclesiastes 4:10 CEV).

People need people. It's God's plan for your life to help you grow and get better and overcome your struggles. It's how you can be healed from your ordeal.

The Bible says, "Confess your faults to each other and pray for each other that you may be healed" (James 5:16 NIV). What do you need to be healed from?

If you want to be healed from an addiction or a bad habit, the secret is this: Don't repress it, confess it. Confession is good for the soul. Grab a trustworthy friend and reveal your feelings. Revealing your feelings is the first step toward healing. However, hiding your hurt will only keep you down in the dirt. What can the dirt do for you? You solution is not in the dirt but in revealing your hurt. The devil will try to get you to keep your struggles a secret. Don't keep them a secret. Grab friends and share your secrets. Make sure they are the kind of friends who will not share your secrets. Make them confess that they will not tell your secrets and that your secrets are safe with them. Any secret will remain a secret until the secret is revealed. Once it's revealed, it is no longer a secret.

For many, they want you to think that everything is hunky-dory when in fact it is not. This is the time when pride is in control. Pride is not on your side. Again, I'm here to tell you, pride is not on your side. You need a friend! When we share our burdens with one another, we can draw from one another's strength and we can be edified. We are not solitary people. Man is not isolated. Isolation has never been God's plan for liberation. Obviously, we are stronger in numbers. We are most effective when we come together in numbers and share our secrets, wisdom, talents, and ideas. Confession works against the worst part of human nature—the part that imagines it to be better than it really is.

C. S. Lewis said, "No man knows how bad he is until he had tried very hard to be good." What's in your life that you are afraid to talk about? Don't let your problem eat you away! Grab a friend and put it in the wind!

Pray for Help

Prayer is communication with God the Father. Prayer has power of everything. God can intelligently act in any part of your life or the universe. Although some people think prayer is a waste of time, the Bible says that the effective, fervent prayer of a righteous man avails much (Jeremiah 5:16). Perhaps they should check themselves or check their God. Who are you praying to? Prayer meets inner needs. One who prays will receive the help they need (Psalms 138:3).

Most positively, God has promised to answer our prayer when we believe that we will receive what we ask (Mark 11:25-26) and when we ask in Christ name (John14:13-14).

There's power in prayer. When you fail or refuse to pray, your power goes away. People who don't pray apparently don't need help. If you need help, look to the hills! Your help comes from God (Psalms 121:1).

Heaven has a twenty-four-hour emergency hotline. And the amazing part about this is every person in the world can call at the same time and still get an open line. God knows what we all need even before we ask. Isn't that amazing? The Bible says, "We have not because we ask not." A person who refuses to pray is like driving their car on empty. You know you need to fill up, but you keep passing every gas station. That's insane! If you keep running on E (empty), you are going to find yourself all poured out. Your car was designed by the manufacturer to let you know when something is going wrong or when something is about to go wrong. When something has gone wrong in your life, pray! Especially, if you're facing a crisis or if you're in the midst of a dilemma, don't get delirious in the midst of your dilemma. When you pray, deliverance is on the way. God is never too busy for benevolence.

God is always standing by, waiting for us to call on him. He knows what you're struggling with. However, he's patiently waiting for you to get on your prayer phone and call him up and tell him all about it. If anybody can fix it, he surely can.

The Bible guarantees that when you cry out to God with sincere words, you prayers will be heard. God himself faced the same temptation that we do at the time he walked the earth. Jesus understood the significance of prayer. Do you? That's why Jesus was always somewhere, praying to the Father. If Jesus had to pray, what about you?

When you pray, you will develop a relationship with God. He wants you to become intimate with him. Prayer is one of the ways you can become intimate with him. The only reason why we don't want to get intimate with God is because we want to keep indulging in a particular temptation even though we know it's wrong. Giving in to temptation is what keeps us separated from God. However, he still wants us to become deeply intimate with him. He wants to become your best friend. A friendship is not a friendship without a relationship. There's an old hymn that says, "What a friend we have in Jesus."

Jesus said, "I no longer call you servant, because a servant does not know his master's business. Instead, I have called you friends, for everything that I learned from my Father, I have made known to you" (John 15:15 NIV).

The word *friend* does not mean just another acquaintance but a close, intimate, trusted relationship. The same word is used to refer to the best man at weddings.

Friendship with God is built upon sharing all your life's experiences with him. If you have a problem, don't worry about it; pray about it. And if you are going to worry about it, don't pray about it. The world tells you to worry and fret when you have problems. The world says misery loves company, and you should gather all your miserable little friends together and have a pity party. Poor pitiful you, what are you going to do? I'll tell you what you shouldn't do. You shouldn't worry. When you constantly think about a problem over and over in your mind, that's called worrying. God doesn't want you to worry about it, but he wants you to pray about it. Instead of giving up, start praying!

Prayer is similar to lifting weights. The more you pray, the stronger you become. The stronger you become, the better you are able to stand against it. If you can't stand against it, run from it!

Run from It!

Temptation is anything that has the power or the ability to entice you to do wrong. Oftentimes, you will find the devil working behind the scene, trying to get you to do the wrong thing. It's no longer a secret. There's more to temptation than what it appears to be. What you see isn't always what you get. What's good to you may not be good for you. As I have already mentioned, temptation is simply your invitation to the gateway of misery. It's all a setup. However, one of the best ways to avoid that setup is to run from it. People who run from situations are often called cowards. However, if being a coward for a moment will save my life, I'd rather run to flee myself from trouble. Running from some things does not mean you are weak and lack courage. If a grizzly bear were about to attack you, what would you do? If you don't run, that bear is going to have himself some fun. Run, Forrest, run!

One of the best ways to defeat temptation is to run from it. Even if that means getting up and changing the channel on your TV from a dirty scene or breaking up with your boyfriend or girlfriend who's trying to get you to do the "wild thing." Moreover, if your passion is burning for each other, Paul said it's best to get married and then *get a room* (1 Corinthians 7:9).

Joseph found himself running from Potiphar's wife when she began to flirt with him (Genesis 39:7). She became infatuated with him and tried to entice him to do the wild thing (copulate). But he refused. When he refused, he was falsely accused, which caused him twelve years in prison. Joseph was a handsome and good-looking man, which is most women's favorite combination. But he didn't let that go to his head. However, that woman was trying to get in his head.

The Bible says she began to cast those big pretty eyes upon him while trying to seduce him and said, "Lie with me." But he refused and said, "My master has given me access to everything in his house except you.

In other words, you're off-limits." At this time, Joseph was second in command to the mighty pharaoh in power. But that didn't stop that desperate housewife from pursuing Joseph daily.

One day, when Joseph was home alone, she caught him—or should I say grabbed him—and commanded him to lie with her. Obviously, this woman was used to getting what she wanted, but not that day. Joseph broke free and ran, leaving her standing there with his coat in her hand. Suddenly, Joseph became MIA (missing in action).

Men! How many of you would have done what Joseph did if you found yourself in a similar situation? Running exemplifies what we all should do to avoid or defeat temptation. Like Joseph, sometimes temptation will catch you unaware or by surprise. It's not a sin to be tempted, but it is a sin to give in to it. Temptation is your invitation to a world of frustration. Martin Luther said, "You can't keep a bird from flying over your head but you can keep it from nesting on it." Who's been messing with your head? Is it a man, a woman, a boy, or a bird?

The scripture says, "Run from anything that gives you evil thoughts and everything that messes with your head . . . but stay close to anything that makes you want to do right" (2 Timothy 2:22(LB).

Running away from temptation is undoubtedly one of the best things you can do to defeat or overcome temptations. However, if you hang around, you will go down. And you may not be able to get up.

Wise people realize that moving themselves out of a tempting situation can be the best move to make. Knowing when to run is as important in spiritual battles as knowing when and how to fight (1 Timothy 6:11). That's right!

Although God may order our various circumstances, he will also give you the strength and guidance to overcome them if you believe. Divine principles have always been the cutting edge for every problem.

Part Four

You Are What You Eat

Many Americans have a bad habit of eating bad. If you are what you eat, then what are you? Wait a minute! Hold that thought! What if you were eating something that was literally killing you? Would you change your diet? If you are what you eat, then you should watch what you eat because what you're eating may be killing you. Many people are not aware of what they are eating these days. We are eating more toxins and chemicals and pollutions than ever before in history. We have gone coo-coo for chemicals. Why? I'll explain later.

In America, as opposed to many other countries, nearly everything you put in your mouth contains some kind of toxin. That's because it's man-made. Truth be told, you should abstain from everything that's man-made. Information is only useful when it is used. Use it or lose it.

Consider this: For years, medical science has duped us to believe that they are desperately searching for a cure for cancer while at the same time, the food and drug industry feed us poison. That's insane! If you are what you eat, then that means you're a person on poison. Medical science has literally failed in the area of curing and preventing sickness and disease. Today, more people are getting cancer than ever before in the history of this nation. Here are some more startling facts:

- More people have diabetes than ever before in history.
- More people have heart disease than ever before.
- More people have acid reflux than ever before.
- More kids have attention deficit disorder than ever before.
- More people catch cold and flu than ever before.

- More people have multiple sclerosis, lupus, asthma, migraine, backaches, joint pain, and neck pain than ever before, and there is a reason as well as a solution.

What's wrong? Medical science has failed. We are losing the war on cancer. The percentage of Americans dying of cancer today is staggering. Americans spend over two trillion dollars a year on health care only to end up getting nowhere. That's insane!

An unhealthy lifestyle means more illnesses and more expenses to treat those illnesses. That means a bigger burden on our health care system. Sickness means more time lost from work, less recreational time, and a shorter life span. However, changing your unhealthy lifestyle means you will lower your risk of all these diseases mentioned. What you put into your body has tremendous effects on your looks, how you feel, how you act, and of course, your life span. You have a better chance of surviving by taking charge of your own health. You can do that by making the necessary changes in what you eat because you are what you eat.

What's Eating You?

What's eating you? I don't mean to be comical. But if you look close enough, you could see what's eating you. However, many of your numerous, tiny invaders are being held at bay by your valiant immune system and white blood cells. They are not just fighting your unwelcomed host of invaders, but your ill-chosen diet and careless lifestyle as well.

It is estimated that 90 percent of all ailments that plague the human body start in a toxic and congested colon. Toxins from a congested colon can weaken and stress the heart, causing pain and stiffness of the joints, tiredness, skin blemishes, psoriasis, acne, and more. These toxins can enter the brain, according to research, and cause senility and abrupt and violent behavior. So the sensible thing to do is to clean the colon. Most people's colons are in even worse shape today than it was in the turn of the century.

Many diets are low in fiber, and waste materials constantly accumulate because of these glue-like foods we ingest daily. However, eating healthy, getting proper rest, and regular exercise will help eliminate waste and keep you healthy. A healthy colon and intestine is essential in order to heal and protect the body from unwelcomed invaders such as cancer, obesity, heart disease, high blood, germs, viruses, toxemia, and more. But when there is a delay in the movement of toxic waste materials along the digestive tract, autointoxication can quickly develop. Constipation is the main cause of fermentation or autointoxication. The main causes are lack of fiber, eating too much cooked food and not enough raw food that contain live enzymes, eating white-flour products, which act like glue in the colon, and a lack of exercise.

You must realize that being sick is not the natural state of the human body. God designed our bodies to be healthy, to fight off germs, toxins, viruses, bacteria, and other harmful invaders. If your body is losing the war, it is no longer in its natural state. You get sick because you caught something or something caught you. It is because your body is out of balance and your immune system is too weak to fight. Even if you don't like to fight, you should keep your immune system in shape to fight.

Keep in mind that being sick is not normal, and it is not the normal state of the human body. Your body is not supposed to get sick and remain sick. If you get sick, it means something contributed to the cause. Think about this, animals in the wild never get sick. Animals in the wild never have heart attacks, why? Animals of the wild have different diets from us human beings. Animals of the wild are not exposed to man's deadly diets, drugs, and human-processed foods. Therefore, they can continue to run wild, free, and healthy for years to come.

It was René Dubos who discovered that a biological organism has a sociological behavior. It was his observation and his contribution to the twenty-first-century knowledge that a biological organism lives in its own sociological environment, and if you change the environment, you kill the organism. It would become what he called a deviant struggling to survive.

Whenever man changes or removes something from its natural environment, the adjustment is always in a downward movement.

What's eating you? There are some things you shouldn't eat because they can turn and eat you, such as shellfish and pork. Let's start with the shellfish.

Most people are allergic to shellfish more than any other food on the planet earth. Why? Because it has no scales or fins. Scales and fins serve as a protective barrier from absorbing toxins. You can actually die from eating shellfish. Any fish that does not have scales should be avoided by all means necessary. This includes clam, shrimp, lobster, crab, squid, eel, catfish, shark, bats, cats, and things like those. Pork is another highly toxic food. A pig eats anything in its path, including its own feces. Whatever it eats grows into the meat on its bones. All pork products are laced with disease and viruses. Pay attention to what you're eating because it may turn and eat you. Many people will eat what God has forbidden them to eat and then turn around and complain about how bad they feel and how bad they are hurting. It is simply a sign of their selfish will. A selfish will can kill. A selfish will can get you into more trouble than you can shake a stick at. Imagine that. A self-willed individual insists on doing things their way as opposed to doing things God's way. We must learn to say, "Not my will Lord, but Thy will be done." We must learn to move our will out of the way. But if you're the kind of person who always wants to be in control and does things your way, like Humpty Dumpty who sat on the wall, you're going to have a great fall. And only God will be able to put you back together again. Think about that. In fact, there are some people just like that. They have to be broken into pieces just to get their attention. They are so stuck on doing things their way that they don't see any other way beside theirs. Just like everyone else, God allows things to happen for our good. There may have been times when you could have died, but God stepped in right on time. Accidents are simply incidents in God's plan for your life.

Every day of your life has already been preset or predestined. Regardless of the cause, none of your troubles could happen without God's permission. Think about that. You can tell people, "You shouldn't eat that," and they will look at you like you have lost your mind.

Don't Eat That

If you are concerned about preventing or protecting yourself from diseases, you should start by considering what you put in your mouth.

I believe Jack Lalanne said it best when he said, "If it's man made don't eat it." Jack Lalanne is in his nineties, full of vitality, healthy, and still going strong. I want to say it another way: if it's man's diet, don't buy it.

Have you notice the word *die* in the word *diet*? Eat the wrong diet; you will die much sooner. Anything that is all-natural or organic is what you should be looking for because it doesn't get any better than that. If something is already in its best state, it cannot get any better than that. So why do they call some products *diet*? Here's why: they want to brainwash you into believing that those particular products contain less sugar and will help you lose weight. Bologna! I have discovered that everything labeled *diet*, especially diet soda, contains a dangerous chemical that goes by the name aspartame—an artificial sweetener. What do you think artificial means? It means something man-made or anything that's not natural. Diet sodas are now called the new crack because they destroy the central nervous system, causing depression, weight gain, and they are highly addictive. How do I know? I used to drink them until I found out that I was drinking poison. They cause a variety of medical symptoms that will eventually call for medical attention. The idea that diet products have fewer calories and are good for weight control is an all-true lie.

The word *diet* simply means the kinds of foods we consume on a daily basis. However, man has given diet a whole new meaning. We need to stick to the true meaning of the word *diet*. We have developed such a skewed, unfettered view of the word *diet* that we don't know whether we are going or coming, losing or gaining.

What you put in your mouth should be as close to natural as possible. If it's man-made, that means it's artificial. Think about that. Why would anyone want to eat anything artificial? Unfortunately, many people are not aware of what they are putting in their mouths. Wait a minute! Before you take another bite, you should examine or analyze what you are about to feed your temple.

Most illnesses, if not all, are self-inflicted. That's right. We do it to ourselves because of carelessness. Now, if you go out and buy an apple, the first thing you should do is to peel it because of the chemical on the exterior of the apple. In fact, virtually all fruits and vegetables have been chemically altered. Why? Because the food industry knows that the more food they sell, the more money they make. It's all about making more money faster than they did yesterday. Any food manufacturer or farmer is in business and has to sell more of their product and produce at a lower cost to make more money. So what farmers do is ask the question, "How can I grow the most apples or oranges or onions in the shortest period, at the lowest possible cost, so I can sell them with the highest possible profit?" Here is the answer: tamper with Mother Nature by genetically modifying what Mother Nature has produced with some man-made concoction straight out of the lab so they can grow bigger products at a faster rate. That's insane; the things that people will do for money is unreal. Money itself is not bad. Only when it begins to destroy the environment and is purposely used to sell inferior products to the public is when it becomes bad. Money should be used, and people should be loved. But because of the love for money, people are used and money is loved. That's backward.

Whatever you eat needs to be organically grown. That's right. You should either grow your own or purchase naturally organic foods. That includes all fruits, vegetables, and meats. And stay away from all artificial sweeteners (including Splenda). There's nothing splendid about Splenda. All artificial sweeteners are poisons and should never be consumed. If consumed, it will slowly but surely consume you. Aspartame goes by the name NutraSweet; however, it is classified as an excitotoxin. Based on research, aspartame is responsible for many distressing medical conditions ranging from headaches and memory loss to hyperactivity in children and seizure disorder. I know that most people are hung up on taste. But it is the taste that kills. Unfortunately, many people are falling for the taste, and the taste is what's literally killing them.

What's for Supper?

I'm reminded of a television show that went by the name *Hee Haw* that was broadcast in the 1970s. On this show, the people would sing and dance and tell jokes while grandpa was in the kitchen, doing the cooking. Somewhere in between, the whole *Hee Haw* gang would ask the question: "Hey, Grandpa! What's for supper?" He may say collard green, mashed potatoes, fried chicken, black-eyed peas, corn bread, ham, and candied yams. Desert may include strawberry shortcake with whipped cream and a cherry on top. As soon as he finished giving them the menu for that moment, the whole *Hee Haw* gang would respond by saying, "Yum! Yum! *Yum, yum* means I want some. Ready or not, here I come."

Throughout history, God has always instructed his people on what to eat and what not to eat. It may not have included strawberry shortcake with whipped cream and a cherry on top, but it was the best thing going on at that time. No, they didn't have a Captain D's or an Applebee's, but they had it going on, considering the circumstances. I can almost hear those Jews saying, "You want some, come get some!" I believe that's John Cena's line, the pro wrestler.

In the beginning, God's diet included every herb bearing seeds and every fruit tree bearing seeds (Genesis 1:29).

As recorded in the Bible, God presented Israel with an unparallel system of laws that if adhered to would have provided peace, good health, and justice for all its citizens. He meant for other nations to see for themselves, including America, the blessing and wisdom that would naturally stem from Israel's way of life and voluntarily choose it for themselves.

The book of Leviticus deals with the dietary distinction between the clean and unclean things. He gave Mighty Moses commands to give to the people relating to what to eat and what not to eat (Leviticus 11:1-24).

Now this dietary plan may seem strange and insane to many Christians. We know that we have been freed from this aspect of the ceremonial law. Paul speaks about this in the book of Galatians and the book of Romans in regard to God's diet.

You must understand that these laws are not primarily being given just for health-related purposes. Some people like to go back in retrospect concerning these laws and conjure up rationales about it, and there may be a lot to learn from them.

Fundamentally, these laws are not just health related. Fundamentally, these laws are moral and spiritual in nature and are designed to create a distinction between Israel and other nations.

As they were moving into a land filled with idolatry, this is the first thing God said, "You're not going to eat what your neighbors eat." Isn't that interesting? So if God, who created you, is concerned about what you eat, why aren't you? Just because your neighbor doesn't eat what you eat does not mean you can't be friends. Answer this: where is a good place to form intimate relationships? Wait a minute! Let me guess—around the dinner table where we gather around and fellowship with one another. What do you think were they doing at the Last Supper, shooting marbles? No! They were developing a relationship. Moreover, God gave them dietary requirements that made his people distinctive in the eyes of their neighbors.

For instance, we find that beef was a big part of their diet. In fact, they regularly had beef for dinner. I believe they had an Outback Steakhouse. It may have been obsolete, but they had to cook somewhere besides a cave. Who wants to cook in caves only to get choked on smoke? Meanwhile, beef was odious to the neighboring Egyptians. When the Lord told his people that they are having beef for dinner, it actually built a barrier between the Egyptians and the Hebrews.

Meanwhile, back at the ranch, the swine was highly favored in Canaan. In fact, for some reasons, the swine is highly favored in America. Hmm . . . I can see why we are one of the unhealthiest nations in the world. However, the swine was forbidden to the Hebrews. So the Hebrews are separated from the Canaanites by their dietary requirements. If you take a closer look at this dietary plan, it would have effectively separated Israel from the Egyptians, the Arabs, the Babylonians, and the Canaanites. It will make you think, something just isn't right.

Other foods that were part of that dietary plan are seed-bearing herbs and seed-bearing fruits, such as the cucumber, cantaloupe, cherries, strawberries, blueberries, blackberries, grapes, muskmelons, watermelons, pomegranates, apples, etc. Other animals included every sea creature that have fins and scales, and some flying creatures, such as the grasshopper and the locust. Hmm . . . I know you are probably thinking that the grasshopper and the locust sound pretty disgusting. However, I'd rather have a greasy grasshopper for supper, if things get bad enough, instead of some of the dangerous foods we are faced with today. The grasshopper is an herb-eating creature. We were created to eat the herbs of the fields, not from some fancy fast-food restaurant. Restaurants purchase their food primarily from large, bulk food supplies that supply hundreds of other restaurants in a given area. Much of the foods at the restaurant don't even get cooked at the restaurant; instead, they simply heat it up and serve it so you can eat it up. And sometimes, it causes you to throw up.

What Goes In Must Come Out

Your body has five gateways that lead to the inside world of the human body. Those gateways are the ears, the mouth, the nose, the eyes, and the skin. These are the five gateways that toxins are introduced or get into our bodies. The major form of toxin that comes in through the eyes is images that cause bad emotions of violent behavior, especially by television and videos games. We are watching more violent movies than ever before in history. Then we want to know why our children are so violent. What goes in must come out. What are you putting in your nose? Is that where all your money goes? One of the most important nutrients to the body is oxygen. A man can live for weeks without food, days without water, but only a few minutes without oxygen. You are already breathing more than enough toxins.

Our bodies automatically produce toxins on its own. That's OK. However, all toxins that are created by the body and put into the body must be eliminated by the body if you want to live. When toxins are allowed to remain inside the body, the immune system begins to shut down. That's why it's so important to have some vitamin C around to help neutralize these toxins. Basically, toxins are eliminated from the body through the nose, the mouth, the urinary tract, the colon, and the skin. These are the five gateways in which toxins are eliminated into the outside world.

The nose and mouth primarily use the lungs to eliminate toxins. Our urinary tract primarily eliminates them through the kidneys and the liver. The colon eliminates them through the liver, the stomach, and the small intestine. The skin primarily eliminates it through perspiration or sweating. I read a quote once that said, "Never let them see you sweat." Wait a minute! That's bad advice.

If your body automatically produces toxins, you shouldn't be loading it down with more toxins. That would only create a more toxic environment at a faster rate. And if it doesn't get eliminated, your temple will soon become a temple of doom. If what's going in isn't coming out, an overload of toxins will eventually wipe you out. It is virtually impossible to avoid all toxins. But you can reduce the amount, which is just as important.

Today we are putting more toxins in our bodies than ever before in history. Our children are being stuffed with this stuff. If your children are like mine, they would eat whatever you put before them. As parents, we are responsible for our children's well-being, including their diet. That's right. If you are allowing your child to eat any and everything, you are literally putting your child's life in jeopardy. If you have been killing you children, it's time to stop. Give them a chance to live by feeding them the proper diet and exercise. Don't allow them to spend their entire childhood in front of a video game. Get them involved in the game of life instead.

Benefits of Exercise

Don't just eat and sleep. Your body was made to move. Your body may be shaped like a Roman god, but if you don't move it, you will lose it! Exercise helps to eliminate waste. In fact, there are benefits that come with exercise. I will get to that in just a moment.

Since people sit all day, especially on their jobs, their elimination process gets congested. The longer you sit, the worse it gets. The longer it sits in the colon, the more it will become swollen. I've heard some people say, "I have not had a bowel movement in seven days." Hmm . . . That is very dangerous to your health. You need at least two to three bowel movements per day to be considered regular. If your bowel hasn't moved in seven days or longer, you are extremely constipated. Exercises, along with a basic colon cleansing, and adding a lot of fiber to your diet will help break up constipation and put it on the run. The longer waste sits in your screaming colon, the more toxins move into your bloodstream. Now you're wondering why you feel so bad. This can turn into a serious health threat. Your elimination process needs to be working at optimal level to stay healthy and feel well. One of the best ways to do that is through exercise. However, many Americans are just too lazy. Instead of walking to the mailbox, they choose to drive the golf cart or their four-wheeler. Now, if you are disabled, that's OK. But if you're not, you need to be shot. I'm just kidding. But laziness is craziness.

Here are six forms of exercise you can choose from:

• Slow rhythmic

   This is mainly walking. Your body was made to move and work. Be sure to check with your doctor before starting any exercise program. Moreover, when you go for a walk, your lymph system is taking in virtual oxygen and is pushing waste materials and toxins out of your body.

• Stretching

   Your body consists of a multitude of muscles, tendons, and long-lasting ligaments. Stretching creates flexibility. However, Americans are the least flexible folks in the world. The lack of flexibility allows negative energy and toxins to accumulate in the body.

• Resistance

   The most common resistance exercise is weight training. However, there are other forms of resistance exercise that are available. Weight training can reshape your body, making it look like a real piece of art. But it does not increase flexibility. In fact, it reduces flexibility.

• Posture

   The most common form of posture exercise is yoga. There are many kinds of yoga. Not all kinds are posture based. Just grab yoga and work with it.

• Aerobics

   Aerobic means involving, utilizing, or increasing oxygen consumption for metabolic processes in the body. By the time you finish a session of aerobics, you will be gasping for air. But it stimulates the entire system.

- Cellular

  This unique form of exercise increases the movement of the lymph system, eliminates toxins, and increases strength and vitality of every cell in the body.

And now, here are the benefits of exercise.

The Benefits of Exercise

1. Increases oxygen to cells

   You are made of many cells. To keep those cells healthy, they need vital oxygen. Most people are oxygen deficient. Cancer and viruses cannot thrive or exist inside a well-oxygenated environment. Healthy cells and proper oxygen will keep you looking young.

2. Movement of lymph fluid

   This system is an important element in the process of elimination. Most people's lymphatic systems are dangerously clogged and sluggish. Exercising increases the movement of lymph fluid, helping with the elimination process.

3. Stimulates cells

   Every cell in your body produces toxic waste. Every cell needs stimulation to rid the body of that waste. If not, it can become abnormal, degenerate, and die, causing tumors, cancers, and degeneration of other vital organs.

4. Opens energy channels

   Electromagnetic energy flows through your body. When these channels are blocked, energy will not flow efficiently. This energy gives life and vitality to all the cells. It serves you well to take care of your cells.

5. Relieves tension and stress

   Stress is a silent killer. Too much stress will put you in a mess. It can be defined in many ways. In simple terms, it is holding in negative energy. When negative energy is being held in, the body becomes open to disease. It can cause muscles to tighten and the body to become acidic. Anger creates stress. On the other hand, laughter opens the door and puts it in flight. Stop being so uptight! Learn how to relax. Control your emotions. If you don't, they will always have you in motion (acting up) that includes going to the doctor.

6. Rest

   Sleep is different from rest. You need them both because together they make your day. Rest, unlike sleep, is simply being inactive. However, when you are asleep you are also inactive. When you are asleep, your body is resting, recharging, and rejuvenating. When your sleep is full and undisturbed, life and energy is being restored. You can rest nearly anywhere, but it wouldn't be wise to fall asleep anywhere. If you don't believe that what I'm saying is true, then don't fall asleep at the wheel while driving. You can end up not waking up. If you fall asleep while driving, you may never wake up.

And now, it's time for me to shut up. I hope I have said something that will lift you up and that will encourage you to keep looking up. And remember, there's nothing you cannot do. You must decide to win. Within the many realms of your life, you will be forced to make many necessary yet difficult decisions; you are the direct result of the decision you have made. You must keep in mind that everything you are is the direct result of the decisions you have made or the decision that were made for you. Like a stone skipping across a beautiful clear lake, each decision that we make initiates multiple ripples. Control your compulsiveness. Be sure that your emotions do not drive you toward destruction. Surround yourself with people who are wise and competent.

Farewell, my friend. I wish you Godspeed, and I wish you a happy and joyful life. May your mind, body, and soul be at rest.

Author's Bio

Greetings, fellow readers! I would like to introduce myself as W. David Sangster, a Mississippi native, born and raised in the small town of Louisville. I am the proud father of five wonderful children, and I am currently engaged to Elisa Ferguson, a New Jersey native. She is a very caring, loving, and warm woman whom I love dearly. As a youngster, one of my goals was to become a professional athlete. However, God had other plans for my life.

Today, I serve as a spiritual advisor and leader. My mission is to positively impact the lives of people across the globe by teaching those methods and strategies for building a stronger character along with a more pleasing personality by impacting the whole person.

As a prophet and ordained minister of the Most High God, I stand as an advocate for freedom, righteousness, and justice for all in these dark days, reminding you that you are more than a conqueror.

I pray that this book has been an inspiration and a blessing to you as expected. May God continue to bless you and keep you as we have discovered the secrets to breaking bad habits.